THE END OF HORSES

Also by Margo Taft Stever

Cracked Piano, CavanKerry Press, 2019

Ghost Moose, Kattywompus Press, 2019

The Lunatic Ball, Kattywompus Press, 2015

Looking East: William Howard Taft and the 1905 U.S. Diplomatic Mission to Asia: The Photographs of Harry Fowler Woods, Zhejiang University Press, 2012

The Hudson Line, Main Street Rag, 2012

Frozen Spring, Winner of the 2002 Mid-List Press First Series Award for Poetry, 2002

Reading the Night Sky, Winner of the 1996 Riverstone Poetry Chapbook Competition

The End of Horses

Poetry by

Margo Taft Stever

Broadstone

Library of Congress Control Number 2022932991

ISBN 978-1-956782-04-2

Text & cover design by Larry W. Moore
Cover photograph *White River Mustangs* © Lynn Butler,
used by permission

Broadstone Books
An Imprint of
Broadstone Media LLC
418 Ann Street
Frankfort, KY 40601-1929
BroadstoneBooks.com

for Cassandra Anais Taft Gomez-Stever

Contents

THREE

ONE

I am sitting on Cincinnati grass.
Horses graze beside me.
Crows sound like children
before the rain.

Galloping Double, Bareback

Down sandy edges of paved
country roads without helmets,
bareback, the sisters clung

to each other, to the horse, to tree-
lined ways that snaked around
and through, as if going somewhere

were not the goal. Their bodies
twinned, hair wind-whipped—the triple
rocking of legs pounding,

the leaping beat of hooves. The girls
struggled to stay the horse
rippling through them like storm.

Wind-battered trees that framed
the hush of birds, silenced
by their galloping—the muddy paths,

the mourning dove, soft-eyed windows
of distant houses. Head down, the quieted
horse ploughed through grasses,

his massive form sleek, willowy.
So much did they long for the beast's
velvet nose to be buried in their arms.

Rabbit Fever

As a child, I contracted tularemia
and almost died because one of our rabbits
kept in decrepit hutches must have
had the disease and bit me.
My sister Kathy and I would let them out
in the tack room attached to our primitive barn,
and we would play among them.
They nibbled and nudged us with their velvet
pink noses and ate carrots from our hands.

When I got older, I became a horse—my hair
the horse's mane and my legs, her legs.
The horse could fly over fields of clover
like a swan, like a goldfinch flitting
among apple blossoms, eating thistle seed.
A horse had the power of late-driven snow,
of a tornado heading wherever she pleased.
She tensed her coat to shoo flies away;
she bolted and whinnied at the moon.

Posture Pictures

In seventh grade, Miss Plemmons, she of the short-cropped
hair, behind the black curtain, focused her camera obscura
on our shuddering profiles, our nascent breasts, as we slumped
forward, shoulders caved in, concealing what was barely there.

The rage in the fifties and sixties—Yale and Princeton took them
along with Mt. Holyoke, Vassar, and the Oregon Hospital for the
Criminally Insane. Later, in class, she informed us the Nazis
had amassed troves of college yearbooks for racial study,

that the tobacco industry paid Professor W. H. Sheldon of
Columbia's Institute of Physique Studies to find that smoking
cigarettes made men more "manly," but discovered instead
it depleted sexual appetites. If she told us about Sheldon's

study of human bodies to predict future achievement and
prevent the breeding of "useless" humans, I've forgotten.
I can still see him on the flimsy photocopy that
Miss Plemmons passed around—his shaved head,

his barely contained rage, that familiar sneer of a man who
would spend his last lonely days reading detective stories,
who believed he could judge people by the outlines
of their silhouettes.

Menarche

My body opens
like a telescope
from bed, always
groping for
blood, for oxygen,
for stars, for
points of light,

for little idio-
syncrasies of light.
Sphere, cylindrical,
press near
my ear, my tongue,
move sinews—
snap, slap,

the skein of skin.
Hawks, dogs,
everything runs
the other way,
the end-stopped rain-
drops, little tablets,
their curved

bellies slap and flop.
Below, the ship
enters—boat,
prow, and bier.
The hill is my bed
and I lie down, seasick—
suddenly, a woman.

Brittle Leaves

The cat scampers towards me,
her jaw clenched—
a feathery object, so

tiny it fits in the clamp
of the tight, sweet jaw
of the one who sleeps

in my bed each night, rests
her furry back
against mine and purrs

a serenity purr.
She drops the intricate
body on the driveway,

the hard, asphalt driveway,
littered with a few leaves,
brittle autumn leaves.

Locked Ward I

Bars on windows framed in black
and keys mean nothing

to the girl who escapes somehow, leopard-
print PJs silhouetted in riotous light.

At McLean's, faces of those
who have outlived their welcome

quiver like struck deer who refuse
to die. Patients, straightjacketed,

slump in chairs; built-in ashtrays
prevent burning, but no one owns

matches. Keys jangle on the attendant's
belt, Christmas bells in July—heat

strains his face, craggy, avuncular.
He unlocks clanking doors—keys

ring against his body. Outside the nursing
station, patients clock

the night, murmur prayers with the pill
nurse, her tray of paper cups a constant

friend—Stelazine, Thorazine, Elavil.
Pills line up, soldiers,

tiny vacation capsules, weaken,
smother them into vacant sleep.

Refuge of Constellations

White moons, satin North
Star, lunar signs, refuge

of whiteness, soughing
the topmost branches at twilight, bells

ring, the changeable sea. Haven
of flowers, red marjoram, lupine,

willows, veils of summer rain, dune
grass protecting margins of land from sea.

Filigree of fragrant gold jessamine,
crinoline, sounds first awakening,

a dwelling you celebrate this wedding day.
Sacred vows, seaside church, love

wakens to the garden of dowitchers,
plovers, the blue-grey dove.

Fertility Doctor

The doctor was in his office, sitting behind his desk. She had asked her neighbor to babysit so that she could rush in after she and her husband, Reginald, had sex. It wasn't as bad as she thought it might be—sex on demand so she could race to the doctors and bare herself for a scraping from which the doctor could make a slide of Reggie's living sperm. She wondered if it were possible to make love anywhere on command—the road, the beach—time and location being inessential to the physical act.

To duck into a closet, an alleyway, a side room, to mate—this was her duty, her only ambition now that she was over forty. She had cleared away all her other impulses just as the housefrau spring cleans her house, she had swept out all her other wants. One day, she woke up with the feeling that she was pregnant, the same bloated sensation that she felt before her first child was born.

It was particularly difficult that day to race into the Kaiser Permanente Office to meet Dr. Kresca, the gynecology specialist assigned to her. Here he was making dire predictions of possible deformation. "Those sperm are unusual," he opined as he leaned over the slide. "They can't swim well. You saw how they travel in circles. We need sperm that swim straight. They have to get in and penetrate that tough crust. I don't think that they'll ever make it."

He was calling her again from the microscope so that she might further examine the slide. She would always remember him there in his long white doctor's garb, his thick German accent, inviting her for a view. "Look here. These sperm are deformed. They are swimming around instead of forward," he said in what sounded like a gleeful voice, even more triumphant than the first time.

They had told her that her chances of becoming pregnant were "so remote that they weren't worth talking about." She wasn't interested in responding to him. She couldn't make sense of the slide with squiggles squirming around in a viscous gel. She wasn't compelled to sit in the bare linoleum office. The waiting room was always so much more inviting, with each patient hiding a story, sometimes letting out brief tidbits.

To her, the sperm seemed odd, unreliable subjects for study with this particular conclusion, especially given the fact that she had already become pregnant, and she had already birthed a child, and especially after her husband had fathered a child in a previous marriage. But they had moved to a new town and consulted with a new fertility specialist after a year of trying, and here she was again beside a doctor waving a microscope like a wand.

The doctor motioned for Reginald to enter the room and closed the door. “Your sperm count is still depressed,” he stated in a flat tone as he stared at the pink charts. “But my wife thinks she’s pregnant,” said Reginald, a confused edge to his voice.

“Must be a false pregnancy,” the doctor retorted without hesitation. “We see that all the time. Women who want children enough just reach for them in their subconscious, and they blow themselves up like pufferfish without having any idea what they are doing.”

In her mind, the microscope protruded from a natural field, the leaves, the inchworms on the thistle bark. She hunched over in the garden planting seeds; she knew.

Quickening

I.

Enshrined inside,
underwater Buddha,
you sit sideways
to the world, refusing
to comply with gravity,
entropy, the messages
of space.

Never still, you bob
in combination with the night—
a bumblebee clinging
to a giant marigold. The bee floats
on high stem, lulled
by wind. Rain
bores him down.

II.

A kiln for child-making,
an oven for gingerbread men...
Jack and Jill, the slow
rumble of their fall, so much
a part of winter, this jumbling
down the hill.

III.

At first the same as cow
or fish, the tail curls
up, a crescent moon.
The bulbous, knobby hands
grasp the moving ground.
Fluid washes against your face, waves
from a breaking sea.

IV.

Invisible under clear water,
interior moons sleep. Clouds soften
the slow rocking. You fold
to suck your thumb, the sound
of your racing heart
quieter than anything
alive outside.

The warming, primeval
underwater world
of the fish is yours.
Voices are muffled, murmuring—
so much is hidden,
dark seeds lodged against dark.

An apple sapling planted
in a hollow stump
blossoms. The unborn
moves, spring winds
return, flowers
bend against the earth.

Lullaby

Sleep, away from
the wrinkled toss

of twisted sheets
and spreading moss.

Sleep, the light grays,
small child,

the torn wind knocks,
rasps, reconciles.

Away from the screeching
gale, sleep

in the cove of
the hundredth

bluebird, sleep.

House Reckoning

I

Through each of the rooms
of his house, he drags his wife
behind him, points to holes
the children made in cushions,
dirt rubbed into rugs, juice
spilled on chairs.
"This is bad," he says, shaking
his finger. "This is very bad.
Soon the whole house will fall
around us; what
have you done to stop this?"

II

She rehearses the games
the children played the day before,
building houses out of cushions,
intricate cities and roads
out of rugs and blocks, spaceships
and farms out of clay
now stuck in the cracks
of the hard, oak floor.

Summer Rain

Nothing delivers me from them.
They will not sleep.
Mosquitoes weave their bodies
through the screens.

They attach themselves
to the undersides of leaves,
their husks litter trees,
shimmering underthings.

Hinges of children's voices
unfold, always hungry.
They suck my limbs, their cries
bind my narrow bones.

The sawed-off edges
of their voices splinter,
crack beneath me.
The house is caving in.

Children crawl and scream,
held inside the eaves
to keep from rain—their brave
contorted faces. Rain

prattles down the spout,
fertile rain.

Death of a Grandmother

You wished to be anyone
but yourself, free
to walk, to make simple
gestures with fingers.
You'd watch yourself on film,
cradling babies, each one
dressed to perfection.
It was always Easter. The sharp
sunrays made you squint.

On film you look tall.
Your husband always walks away,
his back to the camera.
He must be working hard.
Babies are important here—
those who smile,
or smile only
when their cheeks
are rubbed and rubbed.

The neighbors in the house below
note the kitchen window open
for the first time since you died.
Eastern hemlocks glimmer
and twist; the earth is soft
and pliable; loose trees cover
the lawn. Subliminal wind,
shifting body, he sees
you letting go again.

Menopause

The pool they build
in the backyard resembles
a sarcophagus.

A terrier owned
by a neighborhood widower
falls in and drowns.

A frog lives in the water element.
She fishes him out in spring
to take him to a local pond.

She plays tennis with women
half her age who talk
about carpools.

A hawk drops a beheaded, half-
eaten mouse on the front walkway,
most of its entrails missing.

The wrens make a nest
in magnolias in front of her house.
The cats guard the window

inspecting the birds' work.
Cats tremble and chirrup; wings
knock the window.

Beloved Child

From my great-great grandmother, Emmaline M. Fore,
as she lay dying, to her infant daughter.
Cincinnati, Ohio, 1859

This letter traced
by a dying hand, no less
motive could nerve
this sinking frame.
When these lines
meet your eyes, my child,
the mother of your infant
love will long since
have passed from earth.
These words you can never
know the heartbreaking
pang it costs this mother
to utter, unless it should be
at some time your fate
to pass through the same
fiery furnace.

That you have the tenderest,
most discreet of earthly fathers
removes half this trial.
Both deeply mourn
the loss of that friend,
which can never be
repaid on earth. You will read
much of a mother's love,
but will never estimate
what you have lost. That near
friend to whom you have
always poured out your infant
joys and sorrows and whom
in growing years you would have
still reposed on just the same,
you will now let go forever,
unconscious of your loss.

TWO

The shade pulled down
like an eyelid near sleep
rocks back and forth.

Instructions for Mother's Burial

Dress her in blood stone and
azure silk from Le Printemps.
Let blue springs envelope her.
Let her grow roots—a tree,
pulling water from earth

to bough, branches
training leaves; each
season—each separate
body—each universe smaller—
explained and recanted.

Treehouse

Something about roots,
bone-like, tenacious,
that grip the moving ground,
the branches like umbrellas
bent back and broken by the storm,
the leaves' veined references
to hands, and the sound of the wind's
wild working against the leaves...
The boy collected the branches
and stored them under his bed.

Something about the tree seeped
into his dreams, the trunk a hallway,
the branches outlined rooms,
and his family finding shelter
in the boughs, listening
to the sound language of leaves.
He did not see a garden, apples, or any fires.
Everyone huddled together to keep warm.

Molly Sky

The molly sky, the lemons
        in the tree; the molly sky,
                the lemon, the lemon squeeze.
So much more has happened since you left,
        the apple tree,
                the worms have ridden with the red,
the sky is bare and blank.

What is it about birds,
        their bodies rounder than ours,
                and their wings
so certain of flight,
        so clear of the tangled wind?
                The hawks with bells on their tails

gird the highest trees,
        stilled to spot their prey,
                the treed squirrels, the bunnies
startled from the thicket.
        Everything that moves is game.

Bird feathers are straighter
        than an arrow, straighter
                than a tree.
The ocean is the sky
        and you are me.

Leaves hang like fish,
        loaves on the tree,
                autumn brown,
                        ground out.
Hang like little faces,
        hang like faces,
                past faces hanging
                        from the tree.

Barefoot Clearing

Outside, troubled
family spills
over the driveway

that I walk down,
barefoot, kicking
my toe against

each stone
firmly lodged
in its own cement.

Catalpa leaves
dampen my arms,
and a clearing

appears halfway
between my eyes
and the moon.

Dolls

The dolls wait for the children
to wake up. They lie on their backs,
staring upwards as though

the ceiling were a resting place.
For them, love is what counts—
holding them, talking softly,

making certain they sleep
comfortably in their beds.
Knowing how to dress dolls

is an art—just what color socks
each takes, like pouring tea, how
many gowns, where the shoes go.

Dressing could take all day, or
just a second. Dirt sticks
to a doll. Remember, rain

is not right for her. Exposure
to the elements breaks down
a doll's resistance. Wait

until storms abate before leaving
with your doll. Time means nothing
to her. She will wonder

about rain, about everything
trains bring. Tree flowers drape
light strands like spider babies

in soft wind. Dolls are restless
on their feet all day, listening
for helicopters. They gather

on roads after rainfall to smell
the concrete getting wet,
the newly soaked pavement almost

drunk after a dry spell. Dolls
on boats head for rocks
in high winds. How many times

they wished the boat could reverse,
but before motors were invented,
everyone jumped ship. Each day,

supermarket racks sport headlines—
dolls gone sour, dolls born with beards,
hair grown with snakes, Medusa-like.

Gall

Every night, the dream
forgotten taunts
the dreamer through
the day, *remember me,*
remember me.
The crabapple found
on the sidewalk has
no worms—only
black spots, eggs
of an unknown insect.

The fish mouths,
scales, nibble
of the night's edge,
nettle the underwater.
Small bandits,
inaudible, live
in walls. They
remember voices
but never names.
Come back,
come back.

Just when a boat seems
to sink with all hope
lost, a wash
of sunlight, a raindrop
on an eyelash,
an awakening.

Something begins
to flow, water
from the faucet,
dripping leaves
browned in autumn;
galls rise, round,
circular, full of
next year.

Slug Traps

When raccoons begin
their nightly rounds
rummaging
through the fillings
of garbage cans, slugs quit
the dark undersides
of leaves, leaving the emperor
beetle, the common
worm, for the sleek
surfaces of lettuce.

Snails without shells,
sliding along the earth
and its roots,
these cumbrous gypsies
house a human frailty,
thirsting for
an unknown odor,
a formless state.
On a pie plate

full of Pabst,
from all corners
they converge,
forsaking their tracks of slime.

Birds at the Zoo

The urgency as Inca terns
fly about as if their only
thought is getting out—
startles those unaccustomed
to such struggle.

The double-wattled
cassowary takes another
tack and freezes still
as statuary in multicolored
contemplation of her lot.

Rats

The mother keeps lights on
above her baby's crib; the lights
disturb the baby's sleep

but keep the rats away, their teeth
from tearing her baby's skin.
She heard them rattling above

her head; once she saw a rat's
pink snout, another's tail
through the ceiling's hole.

The tail hung down,
swayed back and forth, as if
tempting her to pull.

Rats teemed—night rats flocked
in and out of streets, tempted
by broth, by vats of soup, stirred

like witches' brew. She couldn't
get the rats out of her head. They
gnawed at her brain like cheese.

Beauty Parlor

A pedicurist clips a hangnail
from a client's big toe while Monsieur Marc,
cultivated Belgian, whittles away at her hair.

He praises her botox—only five
injections—her face now full and taut.
In 1905, "blondined" hair was scandalous.

Over a century later, I'm trying to make mine
as platinum as possible—bleach out, then blend with
the gray growing in, cut down on visits and cost.

While I stamp out signs of age, my stylist,
a striking woman who was recently a man,
talks about her boyfriend in a soft, masculine voice.

On the corner below, at Lex and 28th,
we observe a woman, blond hair straggling—
like Marilyn's on her way down—

but this woman's roots have grown in, three inches
of black. "What a shame!" exclaims Monsieur Marc.
The woman stumbles, gropes the trash can—

body bent over, off balance. Oddly leaning, she careens,
wobbles into the street. Bus brakes screech.
She hawks green phlegm.

"Must be on crack," says one client.
Monsieur Mark wonders, "Why doesn't she
do something with her hair?"

Citizen's Arrest

In 1968, my mother drove up fast behind the unwitting Ohio villagers, blowing her horn as if her life depended on it, intent on coercing the people ahead of her into pulling over. She was married to the mayor of Indian Hill, and she granted herself the authority to make citizens' arrests. Her subjects usually cowered in their seats, stunned by the blare of her horn, the intolerable blasts.

High school senior, I cringed in the passenger seat, pretending that I didn't exist—that I was paralyzed and dumb. The drivers either could have sped up to evade her or pulled over to figure out what was going on.

But each time that spring, they warily steered their cars to the side of the road, and my mother accosted them with her scream. *My daughter is attending college this fall.* She often prefaced the statement with *Do you know who I am?* I never understood her question. Perhaps she asked because her manic-depression made it difficult for anyone, including herself, to know her.

Years later, one of the couples she had arrested walked over to talk with me after her memorial service. They had moved out of town; they had traveled back from so far to attend the service.

Back from L.A. with the C.I.A.

She is Angela
Davis's double,
driving back
from California
to Ohio—
even Stuckey's
tries to sell her
poison Coke,
and the fine print
of '60s newspapers
is a code few
have cracked.
The television
talks back.

The man in
the car behind
smokes
a cigarette,
flutters it
from his window
like a sign.
His skeletal teeth
jut out; his white
clothes flow
over craggy bones.

At home, she reads
in *Time*, the army
has gone mod,
and her cousin
has cut his hair,
a sure
sign of defection.
She can't stay
and drives out

of town in circles.
Buffalo
is the only
place to go
even though
the car is bugged.

Bomb Shelter Explosion Report

Sputnik circled the earth; people imagined atomic bombs. Russians blasted Yuri Gargarin into the cosmos—the space race, the new now. Soviets placed nuclear missiles in Cuba.

> Police Report, November 11, 1967: Explosion occurred in underground bomb shelter, 300 yards north of main residence, thirty feet east of garage. Fuse box found near victim's left hand. Object partially covered with blood.

Kennedy ordered, "fallout protection for Americans
as rapidly as possible. We owe that kind of insurance to
our families," October 6, 1961. He asked Congress
for $100 million to construct shelters.

> Mr. Taft's wife called to report the bomb shelter blew up. Her husband, Hulbert Taft, was inside.

Soviets tested the first atomic bomb. Some Americans dug shelters at night to keep neighbors from knowing. A cartoon turtle, Bert, urged children to *duck and cover*. Bomb shelters sold like hula hoops. Newspapers reported radiation readings next to the day's weather report.

> Officers Miller, Hiatt, Wiebold, Arthur, Brakvill, Schlie, and Gruenmaier responded. Upon arrival, they went directly to the location. The shelter was demolished, the roof caved in. Sod, dirt, and chunks of concrete scattered all around. Some white smoke drifted from the southwest corner, and also, from the entrance door. Dirt and sod were blown about one hundred feet.

Russians warned, "It would take really very few multimegaton nuclear bombs to wipe out your small and densely populated countries and instantly kill you in your lairs." Because Gamma rays travel in straight lines, entrance ramps were built at right angles. Blast doors would pillow the shock wave of a nuclear blast and regained their prior shape.

> Mr. Taft had parked his car, a yellow Pontiac Firebird, in front of the barn, directly west of the shelter. Dirt from the explosion was on top of the car. The shelter looked like the roof raised, then fell on the floor. A small area along the north and west wall was not completely caved in.

The Snyder shelter designer spec'd sand floors so dwellers could bury turds and piss. Shelters included battery-powered radios, lanterns, sleeping bags, cots, chemical toilets, heating systems, fuel tanks, firearms (to keep neighbors out). Necessary supplies included bottled drinking water, first-aid kits, reading, writing, recreational material, cleaning supplies, and clothing.

> Officer Arthur checked the blast areas but could not find the victim. The Fire Department responded, along with all available men from the Service Department. Men started shoveling dirt from the roof.

On TV, people watched *Leave It to Beaver*, *Father Knows Best*, *Ozzie and Harriet*, and apocalyptic movies—*On the Beach*, *The Last Man on Earth*. Wall Street predicted the bomb shelter building craze profits could increase to twenty billion.

> The fire department tried to put out smoke from the southwest corner. An electrical fire commenced and arced with water until someone pulled a switch in the house.

Survival stores sold atomic bomb protection outfits. General Foods and General Mills advertised dried shelter meals. A worried farmer in Iowa built a fallout shelter for 200 cows. Salaried spotters searched for suspect objects in the skies.

> Carter Construction Company responded with two backhoes to remove dirt and gravel from the caved-in roof. White smoke had an odor assumed to be propane gas. The caretaker, Mr. Liming, located the underground tank and turned off the gas at which time the white smoke ceased.

Some clients forced contractors to construct shelters at night.

> The backhoes arrived at 5:00 p.m. and the body of Mr. Hulbert Taft was located ten feet from the entrance door, four feet west of the front interior wall. The body was face down with the head toward the south. His left foot was pinned under a large I-beam. His clothing was partially burned, and he was bleeding from his head. Near his left hand lay the electrical circuit breaker with blood on it, and a small wrench was nearby.

Teachers at odd moments screamed, "Drop," and students hid under desks. Banned from going to the bathroom, many children wet their pants.

> The Hamilton County Coroner was advised to move the body to the county morgue. Dr. Victor Strauss, the family doctor, was at the scene. Taft was pronounced dead by Strauss. His body was examined by Dr. Adriano who found the victim had been in perfect health prior to death. Taft suffered a crushed chest and head injuries; apparently, he died in the explosion as determined by lack of carbon monoxide in his lungs.

The U.S. government cautioned that flimsy shelters could burn inhabitants *to a crisp* or crush them *like grapefruits*. Conelrad (Control of Electromagnetic Radiation) broadcast advice suggesting two weeks of food would allow for survival from a nuclear bomb. Each adult could take 130 mg of potassium iodide a day and each child 65 mg to bolster thyroid glands against deadly intake of radioactive iodide.

> At 11:00 a.m., November 11, 1967, the reporting officer, Patrolman Miller, interviewed three girls—Pamela Baker, age 8, her sister, Gillian Baker, age 7, and a friend, Becky Thompson, age 8, who were at the Taft residence at the time of the explosion. The Tafts had recently acquired a small pony. The girls were looking at the pony when the shelter exploded. Mrs. Baker, their mother, advised of heavy concentrations of dirt in their hair, but they were not injured by the blast.

Life Magazine praised a couple who spent their honeymoon in a bomb shelter. One individual lied to his neighbors, stating that his shelter was a wine cellar.

> The arson investigator, Mr. Peterson, thought that the mixture of gas and oxygen at the time Mr. Taft entered the shelter had to be at its highest ignition point. He believed Mr. Taft entered shortly before 4:00 p.m., November 11, and smelled a strong concentration of gas. He is thought to have gone over to the fuse box and pulled the main circuit breaker at which time small sparks resulted and the explosion occurred.

In one of the first "Twilight Zones," the protagonist returns from a space mission; everything is destroyed by nuclear holocaust. One human left is alone.

> In an interview, the victim's son and daughter-in-law assured that their father was in good health and spirit. He had only minor problems, nothing that would lead him to an intentional explosion. He checked the shelter every day after work. He had no known enemies.

MIT Poetry Workshop, 1969

for Denise Levertov

At 3:00 a.m., four hundred cops breached Harvard's University
Hall with clubs, helmets, visors, cans of mace. Pushed one
hundred of us into a hallway, crushed and tear-gassed us.

Close to seventy-five injured, one ankle shattered; she would
never take a normal step or run again. In paddy wagons, they
hauled us to the Middlesex County Jail—boys in one cell,

girls in another. In your MIT workshop, you told us
we would meet only in our apartments, never in classrooms.
You wanted to teach poetry to scientists. We demonstrated

against the Vietnam War. When poets possess the ability to write,
you told me, they do not own their gifts any more than people
own land or animals. Poets are vessels from which poems

emerge. Using a pay phone, Mark and I called you from
the protest against Hayakawa during his speech that January
at Northeastern University. You were giving a poetry reading,

but you didn't want to miss the protest; you brought several
attendees to join the demonstration. We witnessed you emerging
from the subway stop, your voice raised against the cops

closing in, your arms waving through tear gas. Police bludgeoned
the young men who accompanied you and dragged them away.
Later, you looked over my photos of the Harvard Strike to find

one for your new collection, *Relearning the Alphabet*. You thought
the image of the students looking out at students looking in
the half-moon window resembled runes of an unknown language.

Electrolux Salesman

The doorbell chimes.
His nose on the window

exhales; a fine mist
clouds the panes. Pink fingers

smear each separate surface clean.
Hairs on the tip of his nose

press on glass; his eyes flip back
and forth—a metronome.

I approach, turn the handle;
the knob presses on my palm.

This much is certain—
he enters hugging the vacuum

like a newborn
clutched to his heart. I consider

showing him the door, but already
he dismembers the Electrolux.

Clockwise around the Chinese rug,
he grates the power nozzle

circling, mashing. He says
this demonstrates suction.

Like a magician with his dove,
he pops the bag out, waves it

through the air, upends it on the floor.
Dirt mounds up like a cow pie.

He sticks his fingers in,
picks out a pinch of dust

and broadcasts it, singing, "Do you
want your child to play in this?"

Pickpocket

For a year he trains in Brazil,
studies the seven bells of the body,
how the pockets ring and ring,
how the pockets sing out
when he touches them.

Around the pay phones in Grand
Central, he walks his beat.
By the way they hesitate, the way
they move their eyes,
he judges what they carry.
He memorizes bondsmen,
brokers, matrons, students,
lawyers, teachers, thieves.
Deft, disconnected, his hands
seldom pause.

He who resembles everyman
prefers men, the pockets
of their outerwear and inner wear
confer more status—treasure
nestled in their bodies, hoarded
in cavities as if it belonged.

He rifles through wallets—
photos, receipts, credit cards,
residue of others' lives.
As he works the station, trains
keep their daily schedules,
the screeching brakes, the grinding
wheels roll hard against the tracks.

Calling Mother after She Died

Always the outsider, on the
edge, no matter where or how,
your refusal to enter

the border of the living. But for
a few faded dahlias by the fence,
I have forgotten what bound

us together, mother to daughter.
Distanced like the spider
swept down from the rafters,

the orb weaver who once
wove her web, wrestling
the fly. As you sat in the garden

among sunflowers and finches
you once fed, I imagine
your mind roaming.

Nothing about you lacked
intensity—forever
burning tree.

THREE

What is this classical pillar
doing in my head?
I never planted the seed.

End of Horses

I write to you from the end
of the time zone. You must realize
that nothing survived after

the horses were slaughtered.
We sleep below the hollow
burned-out stars.

We look into dust bowls
searching for horses.
When you walk in the country,

you will be shocked to meet
substantial masses on the road.
We do not know whom to blame

or where the horses were driven,
who slaughtered them, or for what
purpose. Had the horses slept

under the linden trees? The generals
and engineers pucker
and snore on the veranda.

This Salt Marsh Was Once a Killing Field

Biddeford Pool, Maine

Always on the far edge of the lens,
the snowy egret,

as rows of two or three, we hunch
over, lift binoculars in northern mist.

Hunters excised egrets
as from a seeping wound,

erased almost an entire species
for quill pens, boas, fancy hats.

Sometimes whole egrets adorned ladies' heads.
We trudge through sand; eiders
dive down, ducklings bob

like corked bottles. Dowitchers peck at
pebbles and insects like sewing machines.

Baby egrets abandoned in nests to starve—
plumes sold for more than the price of gold.

Now, herring gulls crowd the rocks.
Fashions change.

Ghost Moose

Searching for moose, the children
run down to the river, calling

the already gone, the forgotten,
to wallow in stench,

the smell of skunk weeds.
Moose calves become ghosts,

rubbing fur, skin, scraping ticks
off on tree bark.

In mild winters, ticks multiply
and multiply, occupy moose calves,

killing them slowly; their mothers
witness starvation from blood loss.

Moose calves resemble ghosts,
tearing fur, skin.

Calves waste away. Wasted
bodies frighten the forest

floor—foresters call April
the month of death.

Blinded

But whoever hates his brother is in the darkness and walks
in the darkness, and does not know where he is going,
because the darkness has blinded his eyes.

John 2:11

Down, down, down, down, they tell you to lie
down in the coal car to find the inky black
mules, blinded by darkness. Eight years old,
1952, with your father; you are his vet tech.
You travel up on the Piedmont Plateau
and enter the Cresson Mine. No one sits up—
the electric wire running above is live.

All aboard for the bottom. Wet or dry, the shaft
always rains, water drains into the sump.
The mule, horse and donkey cross, sure-
footedness of one, strength of the other,
best of both—the burdened beast is the miner's
friend. In dreaded darkness, mules' eyes
like owls' are sharpened by blackness—

eyes that never quit mines until the mules die.
Perpetual night enhances eyesight, blinds them
to daylight. They stable mules in straight stalls, no space
to lie down; steel doors keep rats from infesting grain.
Your father treats sick mules—black lung disease,
mules exposed to crystalline silica dust. Shocked
by the blackened miners and mules, covered from

head to toe with soot, you hold the lantern
for your father. Some miners spend
breaks with their mules, feed them bread
and chewing tobacco. Mules can be taught
anything, but many fear darkness; boy
drivers find some who will pull cars only
when they carry lights to guide them.

Do you remember the Cherry Mine Disaster—
480 men and boy drivers as well as their mules trapped—
259 people died after the electrical system broke down
when cars carrying hay to feed the mules
got too close to a kerosene lamp? Miners tried
to move the car, and timbers supporting
the mine became an inferno.

In the Darr Mine Disaster, 239 men and boys who
worked with fathers and their mules died.
The company allowed the use of open flame lamps.
When coal dust collected in gassy shafts, explosions ripped.
Rescuers punched through the barrier and found dead
fathers embracing their sons, overcome by black damp—
bodies bloated, blood and foam engulfing their mouths.

Once, miners brought a mule named Tim
to the surface for retirement after he had toiled
for decades. At first, they turned him out
at night to avoid the light. At sunrise, all Tim
could do was nuzzle the green spring tufts
until he noticed a cow eating, and he tried
munching grass, his new heaven.

For I Will Consider the North American Beaver

after "Jubilate Agno" by Christopher Smart

For the beaver is the largest rodent in North America and the second
largest on earth.

For the human desecration of the beaver and carrier pigeon ignited the
conservation movement.

For the beaver, a keystone creature, creates watersheds that are hubs of
flourishing ecosystems.

For first, they are supreme environmentalists who provide hollows in felled
trees for the nesting raccoons, squirrels, owls, ducks, and golden-
eyes.

For secondly, the beaver is a symbol of industry and the national animal of
Canada.

For thirdly, beavers have created verdant soil for the farmland in the valleys
of the northern part of North America.

For fourthly, the beaver engineered habitats prevent erosion, reduce risk
of flash floods, maintain water in streams throughout the year, and
fortify trout.

For fifthly, the weight of the beaver pond bears down into the earth and
restores groundwater.

For sixthly, beavers and their ponds, wetlands, and meadows have
provided nourishment to the brown creepers, nutcrackers,
moose, trumpeter swans, and Coho salmon.

For seventhly, songbirds rest upon coppicing willows, and ducks nest
along the edges of their ponds.

For eighthly, by gnawing down trees in dense forests, beavers provide
sunlight and photosynthesis to support food webs; pond insects
shelter in their lodges and dams.

For ninthly, beavers are balletic and ingenious in water, and their transparent eyelids permit them to see while swimming.

For tenthly, the beaver is monogamous and endowed with familial fidelity.

For the beaver's young help care for siblings and assist their parents in repairing dams and lodges.

For their second pair of fur-lined lips allow them to close their mouths in water while hauling and gnawing on wood.

For beavers can hold their breath underwater for fifteen minutes.

For the beavers' four chisel-shaped front teeth perpetually grow to replace that which is ground down from chewing bark, and the outer enamel of their teeth is thick and tinged orange with iron compounds.

For the beaver's fur is waterproof, soft, and warm with 126,000 hairs in a postage stamp-sized patch.

For beaver pelts were a major part of the North American fur trade beginning in the 1500s that was so rapacious as to come close to driving the beaver to extinction.

For early colonists such as the Pilgrims paid bills from England with beaver pelts.

For Lewis and Clark were astounded by the beavers' productive work, and Thoreau deemed them righteous creatures.

For the Blackfeet believed the beavers were their most valuable partners and prohibited killing them.

For in Massachusetts today, lizards and turtles proliferate and fish abound near beaver dams.

For in the Western mountains, beavers' wetlands cover the smallest area,
but the greatest biodiversity exists around them.

For in North Carolina, the endangered Saint Francis' Satyr butterfly finds
safe haven only in beaver meadows and wetlands.

For no other animal besides the human is an equal of the beaver in the
engineering of the natural world.

For in 1948, when Idaho Fish and Game trapped seventy-six beavers out
of Payette Lake in the town of McCall and dropped them by
parachute into Idaho's Chamberlain Basin, all but one survived to
create new thriving beaver communities.

For the beavers' tail contains fat deposits used as energy when needed, as a
rudder when swimming, and as a seat when in repose.

For beavers slap the water with their flat tails to warn their family of
impending danger.

In 2017 to protect their local wildflower attraction on a man-made island in
a man-made lake, a New York environmental organization kill-
trapped an entire beaver family.

Three Ravens Watch

after *Winter Landscape with Skaters and Bird Traps*,
Pieter Bruegel, 1565

If you were a smooth, shiny circle, we would collect
you for our nests, but your bodies shuffle mindlessly
back and forth. You forget when the ice was thin, when
many of you fell through, trapped underneath.

This harshest winter attracts you to skate, to forget
your misery, scrawling patterns in ice. Ravens,
three of us, stand sentinel, noticing
your slow-witted motions, your clumsy sprawls.

From our high perch, we witness eerie cries of brothers
and sisters lured inside your net strung across the trees.
We hear them crash to the bottom, caught on the great awl,
entangled in the glistening awfulness, your web.

Do not forget, you who now skate, that you will return
to your endless winter, bread riots, witch
hunts, old widowed women targeted, and frozen birds
falling from the sky. We know that you want to eat us.

Snow fell in July; men froze to death in September.
Grapes for wine would not ripen. Parasites thrived under
snow and destroyed your crops. You carry your corpses
in carts; your dead litter the ground in rough cloth shrouds.

Branches extend over ice, harbingers of death;
we know that you want to eat us. You also believe
witches cause livestock epidemics, make cows stop
giving milk, create early frosts, and all the unknown

diseases; witch trials can stop bad weather. *Ye griping
trappe made of yrne, the lowest barre and the hoope with
two clickets*, the devil scourge of all the earth. Remember
ice will again be as thin as this diffused light.

Litany of the Sow

"Industrywide, about 10 million piglets are crushed by their mothers each year, according to pig-production experts, and studies have pointed to bigger litters as a major contributor." Michael Moss, *New York Times*

Farmers drug her to birth more piglets
in a cage so small they cannot move.
Her piglets cry out in pain;
bones dig in her skin.

There was an old woman who lives in a shoe; she had
so many children, she didn't know what to do.
It doesn't matter,
nothing she can do.

Fourteen piglets suckle at her teats;
she shifts her body to keep from losing
limbs. Hear her moans,
her babies' bones tear skin.

Nothing she can do.
Under her weight, her *great broken heart*,
sigh of last breaths, the shudders.
Bones of her own, she can barely move;
bones slash into her skin.

They bind her in steel. She cries out.
Fourteen piglets suckle at her teats.
She cannot
move to comfort them.

This little piggy went to market, this little piggy stayed home.
This little piggy—bones broken,
bones dig in
her great broken heart.

Locked Ward II

Two Canada geese and three goslings
crib grass in a corner patch
triangulated by Redcoat Lane,
Tower Hill Road, and the reservoir.

The goslings nip green shoots
in their narrow constriction,
strangulated strip—downy
feathers fluttering in summer haze.

The geese hover over them, protecting
from menacing cars, blurring by
at breakneck speed, drivers cursing
out windows—*pests, vermin.*

They turn their radios up—"*love,*
oh careless love...." But at dawn, no
cars, no noise, all drivers
sleeping, the parents bring

their goslings across the vacant
road to teach them how to swim.

Dance of the Jackrabbit

Jackrabbits by moonlight
jump queerly, in circles.
They leap, turn, scatter—
pirouettes askew. Moonlight
is the force, the jackrabbit
the medium, following language
under the earth. Earth-
worms roll over the words.
The slow sounds steam.

Hum of fur,
of skin underneath,
hind legs thumping, always thumping
against the unforgiving ground.

Ballad of the Dolphin

Ancient Greeks said they should be treated
as humans; their sailors would not kill dolphins.

How I have thought of you
caught in the fishermen's nets—

they would set them to trap
you to catch the tuna

that swam under your schools.
How the fishermen hung

you still alive, upside down—
your cries brought others.

Fishermen grabbed you by
your tails, strung you, and turned

you, head down in water, tied
you to lifting hooks,

and dragged you to the docks. If any
of you were still alive when they slung

you on cement, they stabbed you.
How last survivors churned

the water red, leaping in panic,
waiting to die. In a "good" catch,

it took them three days to kill
all of you. How mothers whose calves

were entangled could not lift them
to the surface. They listened to their helpless

underwater clicks and sighs.
How often I remember the whale skippers

who would radio the location of hundreds
of you, allowing tuna fishermen

to track down your entire pod. Their nets,
deep, foaming, wide,

so that hundreds could fit inside. How they
used underwater sound

to confuse and drive you down—
how many of you drowned.

Fishermen did not want to compete
with you, but killing you was not enough.

How they used the screams
of several to slaughter more.

How one of you hangs from the prow,
still alive, calling, calling.

The Nunnery

Path where
none was before,
nightingale, nightingale.

Mosquitoes dog us
past the nunnery, the picket
fence snakes up the hill.

Swallows
barely visible,
their wings glint

under a narrow
new moon.

Locked Ward III

The snapping turtle digs
between the young
farmers' carrot rows
one wet night, hoping for
a place to lay,

but June brings drought.
The farmers find their rows
disturbed, and the turtle's
framed face sinks
down in the dry dirt,

only her eyes and nose
exposed, seemingly asleep.
The new deer fence had not
kept her out, and now the
farmers' family gathers round.

The same turtle tried
to lay in their greenhouse
the year before, but did not stay.
Next morning, the turtle is gone—
no trace of eggs.

Elegy for a Blue Spruce

Almost all had forgotten or never knew
          the spruce was one of five planted
in spite to ruin the neighbors' view.

          Four died. No one remembered

the details of the feud, the alcoholic
          so full of ill will no one loved him.
For one hundred years the tree grew

          with not much left to define

the edge between sandy earth and beach.
          Only the spruce remained—eagles
and hawks found perches in high boughs.

          Swallows nested in flowing branches.

A young woman married under the tree,
          her whole family gathered;
only weeks later—

          a freak tornadic blast.

The night before the storm she pleaded
          with them, *the spruce needs help*—
maybe severe drought, maybe

          water rising in the bay.

They ran down to the shore to see the spruce
          undone; the regal blue
lay in state, branches curved upwards.

          Sparrows surrounded it in prayer.

Farewell

Good-bye my orchid, how
I have loved you, the subtle dream
of your varying blue colors,
the verdant arc of your stem,
how you are happy
only in certain places, how much
else we have in common no one knows.

Good-bye my backyard
full of palm trees swishing,
bristling, full of tiny lizards
who climb up the screen porch
to bathe in south Florida sun.
Good-bye our two lounge chairs
by the pool where I never sat,
but always thought lovingly of you,
of bathing in the sun.

Good-bye all the mighty bird sounds,
the egrets, the great blue herons,
the anhinga who spread her wings
to dry. Good-bye to the sullen creature
I glimpsed by the pool's edge.
Whether you were a Nile monitor lizard
or Argentine tegu, I will never know.
When I rushed out after the dog's bark
scared you away, I found another lizard
you had chased into the pool, and I rescued him.

As if he didn't know whether he lived or died,
he crouched, stunned and mute in the grass,
but he, too, has run away.
Good-bye, my hibiscus, I have
forsaken you because you couldn't
survive the trip back up north.

Good-bye intermittent showers that pour
from one cloud like a teapot while neighboring
skies remain blue and sunny.
How I have loved you all.

Ocean Birds

Jealous is the night,
the feckless night,
coming over us
as water into sea,
the forceful day's
geography turned black.

Your body is the sea
I float upon, your skin
becomes the waves.
Nothing will ever bring
you here to me, nothing
will ever call you back.

Notes

The chapter break poems, "The shade pulled down," "I am sitting on Cincinnati grass," and "What is this classical pillar," are written by the author.

The epistolary poem, "Beloved Child," is composed from a letter written to her infant daughter by my great-great grandmother, Emmaline M. Fore, as she lay dying.

With respect to "Bomb Shelter Explosion Report," my uncle, Mr. Hulbert Taft, was the grandson of William Howard Taft's half-brother, Peter Rawson Taft. Along with his brother, who was my father, David G. Taft, Hulbert founded and operated one of the nation's first major television companies, Taft Broadcasting. At his death in 1967, Hulbert Taft served as Taft Broadcasting's board chairman and chief executive officer.

About "MIT Poetry Workshop, 1969," it should be noted that San Francisco State University President S.I. Hayakawa spoke at Northeastern University in their distinguished lecturers' series. He was celebrated by Nixon, Agnew, and Reagan for pitting himself against students. Poet and editor Mark Pawlak, a member of Denise Levertov's MIT poetry workshop, writes about this event in his engaging book, *My Deniversity: Knowing Denise Levertov*, MadHat Press, 2021.

For researching the poem, "For I Will Consider the North American Beaver," I enjoyed reading *Eager: The Surprising, Secret Life of Beavers and Why They Matter*, Ben Goldfarb, Chelsea Green Publishing, 2018, and "The True Story Behind Idaho's Parachuting Beavers," Julia Zorthian, *Time Magazine*, October 23, 2015.

In the last stanza of "Three Ravens Watch," the italicized part of the last stanza was taken from *A booke of engines and traps to take polcats, buzardes, rattes, mice and all other kindes of vermine and beasts whatsoever, most profitable for all warriners, and such as delight in this kinde of sport and pastime*, London, date unknown, reprinted in 1590.

In "Litany of the Sow," the epigraph is from the article, "U.S. Research Lab Lets Livestock Suffer in Quest for Profit," by Michael Moss, *New York Times*, January 19, 2015. In the same poem, her *great broken heart*, which appears twice, is borrowed from "Saint Francis and the Sow," by Galway Kinnell (*A New Selected Poems*, by Galway Kinnell, Houghton Mifflin, 2000).

In "Locked Ward II," the lyric "Love, O careless Love" was taken from the song, "Careless Love," (written by W.C. Handy and originally performed by Bessie Smith in 1925) which was cited by Robert Lowell in the poem, "Skunk Hour," copyright 1956 (*Life Studies*, by Robert Lowell, Farrar, Straus & Giroux, 1987).

In "Ballad of the Dolphin," the statements in the epigraph are supported by research cited in *Dolphins*, by Chris Catton, St. Martin's Press, 1995.

Acknowledgments

Grateful acknowledgment is made to the following publications in which these poems first appeared, sometimes in different versions:

A Dangerous New World: Maine Voices on the Climate Crisis, edited by Meghan Sterling and Kathleen Sullivan, Littoral Books, 2019, "Ghost Moose"
A Poetry Congeries, Connotation Press: An Online Artifact, "Birds at the Zoo"
Beltway Poetry Quarterly, "Citizen's Arrest," "Fertility Doctor"
BigCityLit, "Back from L.A. with the C.I.A," "Beauty Parlor," "Beloved Child"
Canary Literary Journal, "Ballad of the Dolphin," "End of Horses," "Litany of the Sow"
Erratio Poetry Journal, "Molly Sky," "Rabbit Fever," "Rats"
Flock: A Literary Journal, "Lullaby"
Folio, "Slug Traps"
G.W. Review, "Instructions for Mother's Burial," first published as "Instructions for Burial"
Harvard Advocate, "Barefoot Clearing," "Shade pulled down," "What is this classical pillar"
I Wanna Be Loved by You: Poems on Marilyn Monroe, edited by Susana H. Case and Margo Taft Stever, Milk & Cake Press, 2022, "Beauty Parlor"
Lightwood: Life and the Arts in the 21st Century, "Gall"
Live Encounters Poetry & Writing, "Refuge of Constellations," "Elegy for a Blue Spruce," "Farewell"
Lumina, "Ocean Birds," "Pickpocket"
Plant-Human Quarterly, "Treehouse"
Mom Egg Review, "MIT Poetry Workshop, 1969"
Plume Poetry Journal, "Dolls"
Poet Lore, "Dance of the Jackrabbit"
Poetics for the More-Than-Human-World: An Anthology of Poetry and Community (dispatchespoetrywars.com) 2020, edited by Mary Newell, Bernard Quetchenbach, and Sarah Nolan, "Three Ravens Watch"
Rewilding: Poems on the Environment, edited by Crystal Gibbins, Flexible Press, 2020, "Ballad of the Dolphin"
Salamander Literary Journal, "Menopause"
Sisyphus Literary Magazine, "Blinded"
Split Rock Review, "For I Will Consider the North American Beaver"
STATOREC Literary Magazine, "Litany of the Sow," "Locked Ward I," "Locked Ward II," "Locked Ward III"
SWWIM Every Day, "Menarche"
upstreet, a literary magazine, "Ghost Moose," "Posture Pictures," "This Saltmarsh Was Once a Killing Field"
The Same, "Death of a Grandmother," "Electrolux Salesman"
Valley Voices: A Literary Review, "House Reckoning," first published as "House Raising," "Summer Rain," "Galloping Bareback Double"

Verse Daily, "Dolls"
Visible Poetry Project, 2020, "End of Horses," chosen for short film by Christina Ellsberg (visiblepoetryproject.com)
West Branch Literary Journal, "Treehouse"

Some poems were published in the chapbooks *Reading the Night Sky*, Winner of the 1996 Riverstone Poetry Chapbook Contest; *The Hudson Line* (Main Street Rag, 2012), *The Lunatic Ball* (Kattywompus Press, 2015), and *Ghost Moose* (Kattywompus Press, 2019).

Thanks to Lynn Butler for the cover photograph, *Wind River Mustangs*, taken in 2021 of wild horses saved by a Navaho family. These mustangs live at the Wind River Horse Sanctuary in Lander, Wyoming. Copyright © Lynn Butler.

Special thanks to Susana H. Case, Suzanne Cleary, Julie Danho, Jeffrey Harrison, and Ann Lauinger for their insightful and generous editing of this collection. I would also like to thank the members of my writing workshop—Marion S. Brown, Sally Bliumis-Dunn, Peggy Ellsberg, Joan Falk, Jennifer Franklin, and Don Krieger—for the astute clarity of their criticism. I would like to thank Larry Moore, editor and publisher of Broadstone Books, for his invaluable input on putting this book together. Finally, I would like to thank my husband, Donald W. Stever, for his brilliance and vision.

About the Author

MARGO TAFT STEVER's full-length poetry collections are *Cracked Piano* (CavanKerry Press, 2019), which was shortlisted and received honorable mention for the 2021 Eric Hoffer Award Grand Prize, and *Frozen Spring*, Mid-list Press 2002 First Series Award for Poetry. Her latest of four chapbooks is *Ghost Moose* (Kattywompus Press, 2019). Her poems have appeared in literary magazines including *Verse Daily, Plant-Human Quarterly, Cincinnati Review, Rattapallax, upstreet, Salamander, West Branch, Poet Lore, Blackbird, Poem-A-Day*, poets.org, Academy of American Poets, and *Prairie Schooner*. She co-authored *Looking East: William Howard Taft and the 1905 U.S. Diplomatic Mission to Asia* (Zhejiang University Press, 2012). She is currently an adjunct assistant professor in the Bioethics Department of the School of Medicine at Case Western Reserve University. Stever also teaches a poetry workshop at Children's Village, a residential school for at-risk children and adolescents. She is founder of the Hudson Valley Writers Center and founding and current co-editor of Slapering Hol Press. (www.margotaftstever.com)